Keyboarding

Any Body Can Learn To Type

New 9 Lesson Short Course

Dr. Katie Canty, Ed.D.

ISBN: 9798693137424

Table of Contents

This is where to begin. Complete this page first.

My name is _____

Start date_____

Planned completion date_____

My teacher, tutor, helper name and email or website

Name_____   _____

My email/web address is

_____

My password_____

Your goal(s)

Are you planning to use your touch-typing skills mostly for personal interests, social media, work, or school?

_____

Your question(s)

Do you have a special question about digital keyboarding at this time?   If so, write it here.

_____

About this typing training....

Mission

Develop and practice good keyboarding digital literacy skills

--a necessity in today's digital world where keyboards are used everyday

Goals

- Practice touch typing via these 9 lessons
- Build digital keyboarding speed and accuracy

Objectives

ABC Objectives – How **A**ny **B**ody **C**an Learn to Type

A. Study, understand, then practice good typing technique for hands and fingers placement, sitting position, and eyes on copy.

B. Practice in the order given **as slowly as you need to** until each word and exercise is completely mastered with accuracy.

C. Faithfully focus practice. If you can, practice 3 times a day for 10 to 15 minutes or one time a day for 25 minutes without distractions.

Resource Requirements

A. This book with printable digital practice keyboards

B. Standard computer keyboard with Internet access

C. Your presence, participation, and practice

Practice Instructions

A. Complete hands and fingers placement Sections 1-2 on paper keyboards.

B. Then, after mastering Sessions 1-2 on paper keyboards, complete Sections 3-9 on a personal computer, laptop, Chromebook, iPad, or other standard digital keyboard.

C. In these sessions, cell phones are not yet recommended for practicing all 10 fingers, good touch-typing technique.

Content

A. Nine short, but good touch-typing training sessions that focus on alphabet keying, a few symbols, spacing, and making capitals – **2 sessions on paper keyboards and 6 sessions from free online learning to type websites**

B. Keyboarding vocabulary, good typing tips, and a new "Did You Know" feature

C. Practice lessons, paper keyboards, assessments, and a certificate

Outcome Expectations

A. Key 15 words per minute or more while demonstrating good touch-typing technique

B. Demonstrate an ability to accurately key names and words, understand basic typing terms, and pass beginner typing skill assessments

C. Earn the keyboarding readiness speed and accuracy certificate by completing Lesson Sessions 1-8

Did You Know?

It is 20,000 years into the future, when the Scottie character from Star Trek saves the day and the planet because he can manually touch type fast and accurate and not hunt and peck.

Much of the world today still depends on 10 fingers, 2 hands touch typing for keyboarding speed and accuracy.

Ready – Let's Begin.

Orientation Session 1

A. Touch Typing Preparation

B. Good Typing Tips – Jewelry and Posture

C. Keyboarding Typing Words

and Terms to Know

Touch Typing Preparation
Getting Ready to Type
Things to Do Now

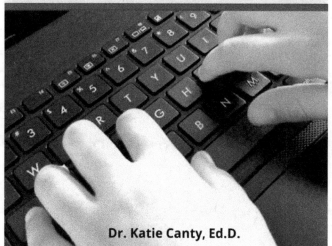

1. Look through this book. Fill in the Welcome page with your responses.

2. Read the information in the boxes on pages 5-7 to understand how this book can best help you.

3. Gather and check your typing resources. Find a comfortable, safe, distraction free place to practice—preferably with a chair to sit in and a desk top or table top surface for the keyboard.

Good Typing Tip - Jewelry

Long fingernails, lots of wrists jewelry, or chunky rings are great for activities other than learning to touch type.

Keyboarding Typing Words and Terms to Know

A. Typing and keyboarding: What's the difference?

The words mean the same thing—writing or entering text by pressing keys on a machine device. Pressing keys to write on a typewriter was called typing. Then, the word typing got an update to keyboarding when computers were used rather than typewriters.

B. Touch-typing: How do I do that?

Touch typing means that you are continuously looking at the screen and not your fingers as you type on the keyboard. To touch type, use both hands and all 10 fingers to type while looking at the screen and not at your fingers. When you touch type correctly, you know the key locations so well that you type accurate and fast.

C. Good typing technique—keyboarding position: What's that about? It is about how you sit, place your hands and fingers, and even what you are thinking about as you type. Note how the feet, back, eyes, and hands are positioned for good typing technique.

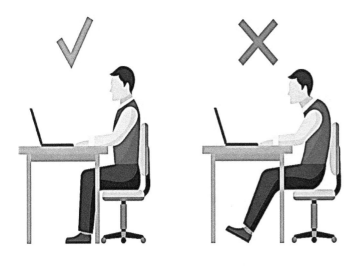

CORRECT AND INCORRECT SITTING POSITION

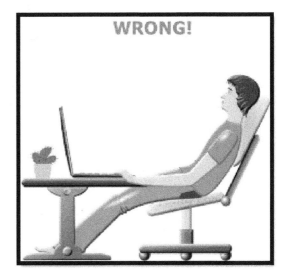

Good Correct Typing Posture

To see what good typing posture correct hands and fingers placement looks like, view a couple of YouTube videos. Choose from video selections like these.

A. Proper keyboarding techniques: **a hip-hop music version**

https://www.youtube.com/watch?v=P_GtjT33urY

B. Keyboarding techniques: **a beginner student demonstrates**

https://www.youtube.com/watch?v=4UJ9BkSbR-I

C. How to Type - Touch Type Tutorial: **amazing transparent typing hands show you correct hands and fingers placement**

https://www.youtube.com/watch?v=MPPG9GbNUg0

Orientation - Keyboarding Readiness Self-Check

Good Typing Posture Practice
Things To Do Now

Place your paper keyboard near the edge of your desk or typing surface. Position your chair so that it is not too close up, or too far away from your paper keyboard. A chair placed about your hand's length away from the edge of the paper keyboard is good.

To complete the orientation self-check, demonstrate good touch-typing technique by doing the following:

1. Sit up straight; hips back in your chair

2. Both feet flat on the floor

3. Elbows at your side

4. Fingers curved over home row keys on the paper keyboard

5. Palms not resting on the keyboard

6. Eyes on this copy of home row keys

asdf jkl;

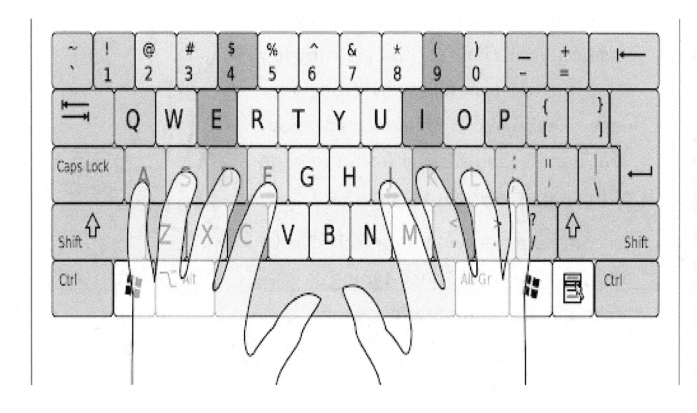

This concludes the Orientation Session.
Date and time of completion goes here.

_____

Grade Summary goes here
OR

A statement of what you learned about keyboarding typing that you did not already know

_____

_____

Did You Know?

Cell Phone Typing Champion

If you type these two sentences correctly in less than 41 seconds on a cell phone, then you beat the world's record for text messaging typing speed.

"The razor-toothed piranhas of the genera Serrasalmus and Pygocentrus are the most ferocious freshwater fish in the world. In reality they seldom attack a human."

Qwerty Computer Keyboard Typing Champion

QWERTY refers to the first six letters on the upper row of the computer keyboard. Today's world champions type at rates over 200 words per minute. One of the champions trained by typing the alphabets backwards and forwards. This site shows how.

https://www.speedtypingonline.com/games/type-the-alphabet.php

You - This Book's Typing Champion

To type fast and accurate enough to be productive on computer keyboards to meet your needs, is that your goal, too? Everyone's goal may not be to be a world champion typist or an above 100 words a minute typist. Most people average 40 words a minute.

Absolute beginners may average 15 or more words per minute upon completion of this training. **Rather than speed, the goal for right now is accuracy using correct touch-typing technique.**

Ready, let's begin the next lesson.

Session 2
On Paper Keyboards

Hands and Fingers Placement

A. Good Typing Tip – Mindfulness

B. Home Row Keys - Correct
Hands and Fingers Placement

C. Digital Keyboarding - Top 4
Frequently Asked Questions and Answers

Session 2
Good Typing Tip - Mindfulness

Learning to type begins with the mind. Help train your brain to remember the home row key locations. Quietly say the name of the key to yourself in your mind as you type it with the assigned finger.

When you practice a lot, fingers will learn to respond automatically and you will no longer need to memorize or think about typing key locations.

right hand a s d f   left hand   j k l ;

Memorize the position of the home row keys for now.

Correct Hands and Fingers Placement
See What It Does and Does Not Look Like

The paper computer keyboard is recommended for this practice session. **Practice three times placing, removing, then placing your hands and fingers correctly back on the home row keys**. Notice that the wrists are not to be twisted or allowed to rest on the edge of the keyboard.

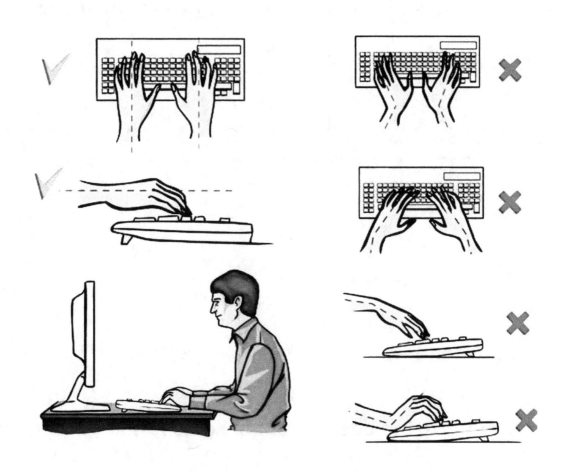

Home Row Position – Left and Right Hands Placement

A. Place your hands in correct home row position by placing

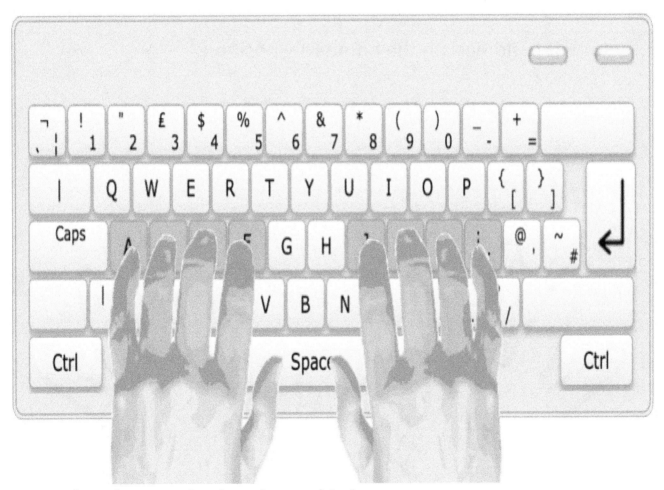

your hands over the hands on this image.

Home Row Keys Fingers Practice on a Paper Keyboard

B. With hands and fingers in home row position, type **asdf** with assigned fingers on the right hand. Press the space bar with the right thumb. Type **jkl;** with the assigned left fingers. Press the enter key with the left little finger. After pressing enter, place your left hand back in the home row position.

Assigned Home Row Key Reach Fingers

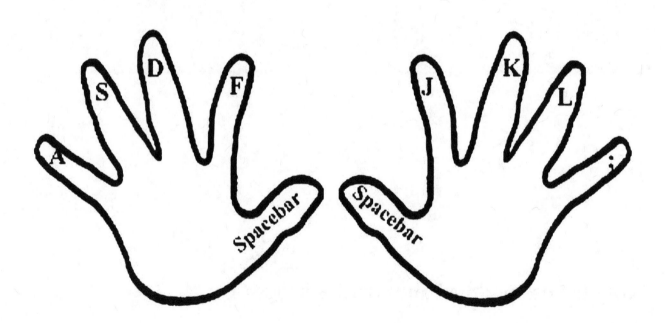

Type each line 2 times —no peeking at the hands and fingers once you begin to type.

asdf (space)	asdf (space)	asdf (Press Enter key.)
asdf (space)	asdf (space)	asdf (Press Enter key.)
jkl; (space)	jkl; (space)	asdf (Press Enter key.)
jkl; (space)	jkl; (space)	asdf (Press Enter key.)

Home Row Keys Practice Paper Typing Keyboard

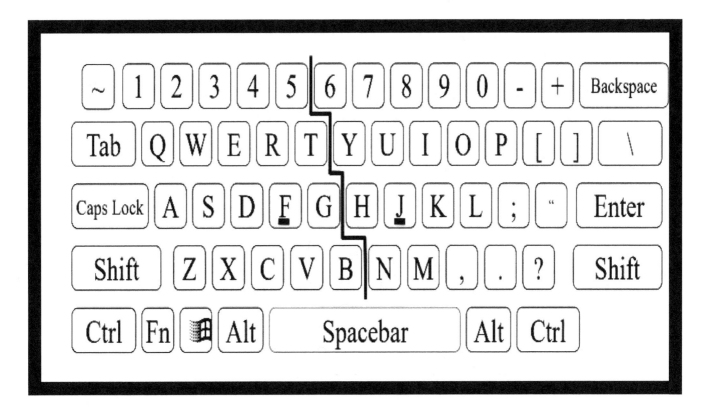

Home Row Hands and Fingers Placement Test

C. To test yourself, practice on the blank keyboard before going on to the next session. When you use good typing technique to type the middle home row keys on a blank keyboard like this without looking at your fingers, you are really making progress.

Type the home row keys forward and backwards 2 times.
Type forward.
asdf (space)   jkl; (Press Enter key.)
asdf (space)   jkl; (Press Enter key.)
Type backwards.
fdsa (space)   ;lkj (Press Enter key.)
fdsa (space)   ;lkj (Press Enter key.)

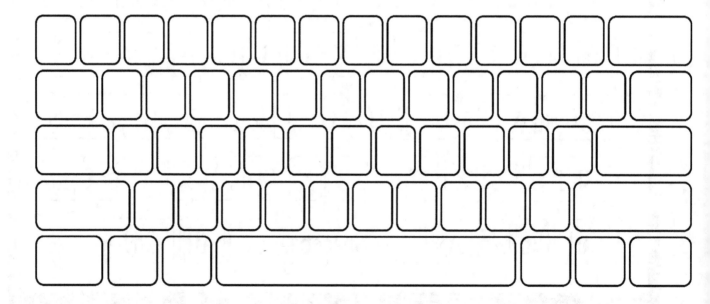

Session 2
Keyboarding Typing Questions & Answers

A. Am I hunt and pecking or touch typing?

Hunt peck typing is a lousy, much slower pace form of locating keys whereby keys have to be located by sight before pressing the keys. Hunt peck typing is also using the same two fingers to locate keys visually in order to type. **Touch-typing** means you look at the screen and not your fingers as you type with speed and accuracy.

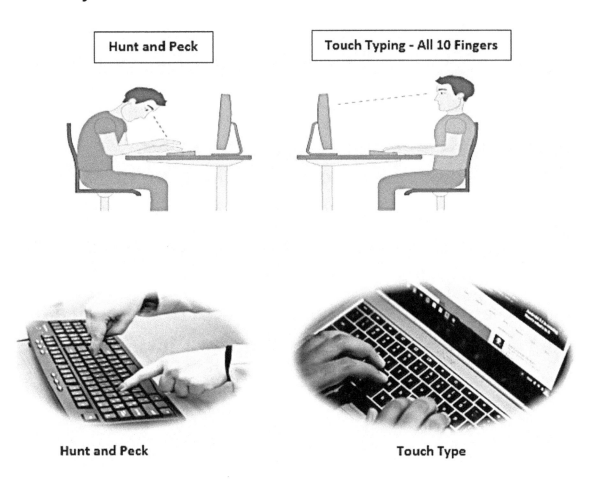

B. Why should I practice on a paper computer keyboard?

Printable paper computer keyboards give you a practice head start on learning correct hands and fingers placement for touch typing. This makes it a lot easier when you do get in front of a computer screen to learn to touch type.

C. People type anywhere and in many different environments nowadays, so why is typing posture important?

Whether standing to type or sitting to type, good typing posture and correct hands and fingers placement maximizes speed and accuracy plus prevents strain and injury.

D. What is so important about home row keys?

The home row is the middle row of keys on the keyboard that you use as important guide keys. The home row keys are a **s d f j k l ;** and there is usually a ridge on the f and j home row keys to let you know where your fingers are. Placing your hands and fingers correctly over the home row keys is what typing teachers call "home row position. **It is of upmost importance to get to know the home row keys locations so well that you do not need to look at your fingers on the keyboard.**

Self-Check Session 2

1. What are the home row keys?

2. According to the YouTube video, what is one of the best techniques for learning to type well?

3. If you would like, place your good typing posture demonstration selfie here.

....

This concludes Session 2.

Date and time of completion goes here.

_____

Self-grading goes here. (Grade A, B, C, D, or work in progress (WP)

____

OR

What do you need to focus on?
posture, eyes on copy, hands and fingers placement, or something else?

_____

Ready, let's move forward to Session 3.

Session 3
On Paper Keyboard and Digital Keyboard

A. Good Typing Tip – Napkin or Coin

B. Make Capital Letters - Shift Keys

C. Shift Keys Practice

Did You Know?

Masses of people work on a digital keyboard throughout a standard 8-hour workday. By using keyboard shortcut keys, there are 8 entire workdays that can be saved every year.

Type Smarter: Shortcut keys help provide an easier and quicker method of navigating and executing computer software commands. For example, the caps lock shortcut key is pressed to type a group of alphabets in all capital letters all at the same time, like HAPPY BIRTHDAY.

Session 3
Good Typing Tip – Napkin or Coins

Both of these are very helpful exercises. Try typing the home row keys with a cloth napkin over the hands so that you cannot see the keys. A dish towel works well, too. The napkin serves as a keyboard cover that gets rid of temptation to look down at keys. Feel for the bumps on the F and J home row guide keys to get and keep your fingers in the right home row position.

The coin typing tip is more challenging. Place a coin on top of each wrists and try to keep it there while you type the home row keys. The coins help to keep wrists low and prevents fingers from lifting too high off the keys.

Session 3
Shift Keys - How To Type A Capital Letter

Now that you know how to correctly touch type the home row—asdf jkl, it is time to move on and learn how to make a capital letter. There is a shift key on the right and one on the left that are used to make a capital letter. Hold down the shift key and then press the desired alphabet key.

Important: The shift key to press with the right or left little pinky finger depends on what alphabet you are typing. Use the right shift key to make a capital for alphabets controlled by the left hand. For keys controlled by the right hand, use the left shift key.

Example: To make the letter A capital, press down the right shift key and then type the letter A.

Note: Shift keys are also used to make a symbol located on top of the number keys. Example: To make the sign at @ used in an email address, press the right shift key, then type the number 2 key. To better understand how to correctly use the two shift keys, view a couple of very short videos on YouTube like these.

Touch Typing Course : How to type CAPITAL letters - YouTube
https://www.youtube.com/watch?v=c92SnYjPE3M

Shift Key/Capital Letters - YouTube
https://www.youtube.com/watch?v=MZFxD_2cMmE

Session 3   **Practice**

Using Shift Keys Correctly Practice
Things to Do Now

Place your hands and fingers in home row position on the paper keyboard here. Practice returning to home row position after using a shift key. Practice each line 2 times.

1. aAa sSs dDd   Press down **right** shift key.

2. jJj   kKk lLl   Press the **left** shift key.

3. Al Ed Dad Lad Sal Kal Gal

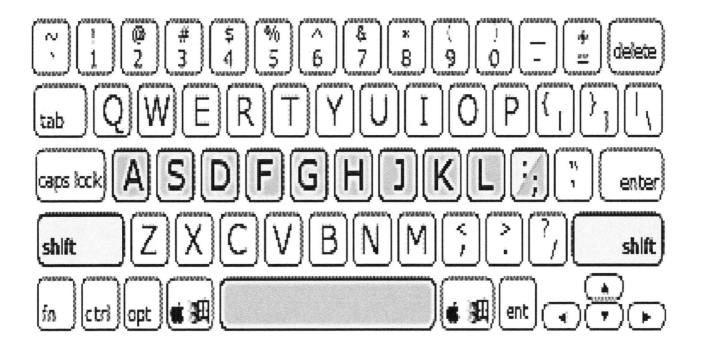

Session 3
Keyboarding Typing Terminology To Know

1. F and J Ridge Lines

The ridges located at the bottom of the F and J computer keys are there to help users find the correct keys without looking down. The reason why only the F and J keys have ridges is to help users place their hands and fingers in the correct typing position.

2. Caps Lock Key - a toggle key that if pressed by mistake will cause letters to appear in all capital letters. To turn off the letters appearing in all capitals, toggle or press the caps lock key again.

3. Text Wrapping - no need to press the ENTER key--text automatically goes to the next line as when taking a typing timed writing test

This concludes Session 3.
Date and time of completion goes here.

_____

Self-grading goes here. (Grade A, B, C, D,
or work in progress (WP)

_____

OR

What song describes your
touch typing skill development so far?

_____

Session 4

Getting Started
Touch Typing
Website Practice

Did You Know?

A school that uses this typing book is called Tech Academy. The academy specializes in motivating and training absolute beginners, the tech resistant, and populations that grew up without using computers.

With their new touch-typing skills, the academy's reformed hunt and peckers are no longer ashamed to type in front of paying customers. Learners benefit by typing their own school papers and preparing their own personal use documents. Individuals who used to be digitally disadvantaged or ashamed of their typing are now able to happily Internet connect with businesses, entertainment sites, and their family and friend groups whenever they want to--without bothering others or having to pay for typing help.

Session 4
Good Typing Tip – Keyboard Keys Coverup

A learn to type blank keyboard skin is a cover that fits over the keyboard and hides writing on the keys. This helps to prevent and/or correct hunt and pecking because there is nothing to see if you start looking back and forth to find the correct keys.

Website Lesson Completion Guide   Session 4
Enter online keyboarding practice website.

- Go to www.typing.com.
- Look for the LOG IN tab.
- Enter your email address and the password.

Suggestion 1 - LESSON COMPLETION: Complete all the lines in each lesson. If a few lines or half a lesson is completed, the software will not save it as a completed lesson. It may take 15 to 18 minutes for an absolute beginner to complete a lesson.

Suggestion 2 - REPEAT OR GO TO NEXT LESSON: Yes, a lesson can be repeated several times. If you are backspacing a lot to correct errors, this is a good indication that a lesson needs to be rekeyed before going on to the next lesson.

Tips for avoiding software malfunction

Tip 1 - CAPS LOCK KEY: If the keyboarding classroom software locks up while you are typing, press the CAPS LOCK key to unlock the software. On some computers, a light shows up next to the caps lock key when it is on. If you press the caps Lock key again, this will start things back working. The caps lock key is a TOGGLE key, which means press it to turn it on and press it again to turn it off.

Tip 2 - RED LINE: This means the keyboard letter needs to be typed in order to move on.

Tip 3 - END OF LINE: Press the ENTER key to go to a new line.

Session 4

Three More Computer Keyboarding Terms to Know

1. Timed Writing - Measures typing speed and accuracy as **GWAM**, gross words a minute or **WPM**—words per minute

2. Semi-colon and Colon - Punctuation marks across from the L key: Key the semicolon with the smaller pinky finger on the right hand. Press the shift key to make a colon.

3. Period - Punctuation mark at the end of a sentence: Space 1 time after keying a period between sentences.

Session 4 Practice Drills To Complete
Typing/Computer Keyboarding Practice Session Diary

Name _____

Lesson #	Completion Date	Start time	Finish time	What emoji describes your lesson typing experience?
J, F, and Space 1				
U, R, and K 2				
D, E, and I Keys 3				
C, G, and N Keys 4				
Beginner Review 1 Self-Check 5				

Session 5

Reaching Out
Touch Typing
Website Practice

Did You Know?

Computer Keyboard Typing Artists

```
        ' ' ' ' '
        | | | | |
    @@@@@@@@@@
    {~@~@~@~}
   @@@@@@@@@@@@
   {~@ HAPPY @~}
   {   BIRTHDAY  }
   @@@@@@@@@@@@
         __) (__
        /_____\adj
```

```
                t:
            :1i:01t:.L      :,
           C8i,1t,1i:1:,,,,,:,
          ..:C08:2it,,,1i01i:,,.:
   .:C:C     :  iL. 0i,,i18ti:,,:
   0:2L:T:T8iiit00:C :t1iii0C:,:,:L
   80000000:,,:,,,::,,i,::i10C:,,::.:
   1tt:C:,,,:::,,,,:,,,,1,,i:T8:C1i,,,0
   C:L:,,,,,:::,,,,,,t8,,,t00:C1i,,:.
   01ti,,,,,,,,,,1,C88:C,,,i1:T1:C0C0:0
   .:t1t:T1iiiii1i0:888,,,,iiiiii
    .80:C1:CC:888888,i:T1iiiiii,,C
    i:C1:C1:C0C0:C:T0r:C1iiiiiii1i,,
    ,C:t:T1i0CC0T0Ttr1i,iiiiiii1ii.
  .C:t1:C1:C: 0:T1i,,,,iiiiiiiiii1C        i1,:
  C0i1:C. ,i:T1i,,,,,iiiiiiii1111iiiC      .ti:C
  C0C1:C0 C1:t1i,,,,,iiiiiiii1trr1i:       i:T,
  .C:C:t1:C C1:t1i,,,,,iiiiiiii1i1i,:,:iC:t      1t,,,
  00T1  1i:T1i,,,,,,,iiii10,::::,iiitit1       :1i,:8t
          8:::t1i:C,,,,,,,,ii:,::iiiiiiii1itit    C0i,:i
          ,C:t:T1i,,,,::,L,:C,::,iiiiiiiiii1iC    .i1,,:C
          1i18::01i,,,::11i1i,::,,,,,,,,iit:T:0   11ri::L
          C:T:C8Cti,,,::0C:t:C,,,,,,,,,,,itt:10T1i,, it
          L,t1i0 t1,,,:1:T00C:,,,,,,,,,1i,,t:C0i:C1i11t:
          C:,it1:C1:t1,,:8080C0C:CL,,,,,,,,,1,t0i1rrrt10,
         :,:11:T1i0011,,,,:1r0:,,,:::::,,,,,,,ttiir,
         1t:C0iL0C0t1i,,,,,:T0i0ii,iiiii1111111tt:C,
              :8L:C0rr1t:C :08C::::C0.
```

People, including a beginner typist, can work magic with
their keyboard keys to create works of art called ASCII art.

Session 5

Good Typing Tip – Correct Hands and Fingers Placement Practice, Practice, Practice

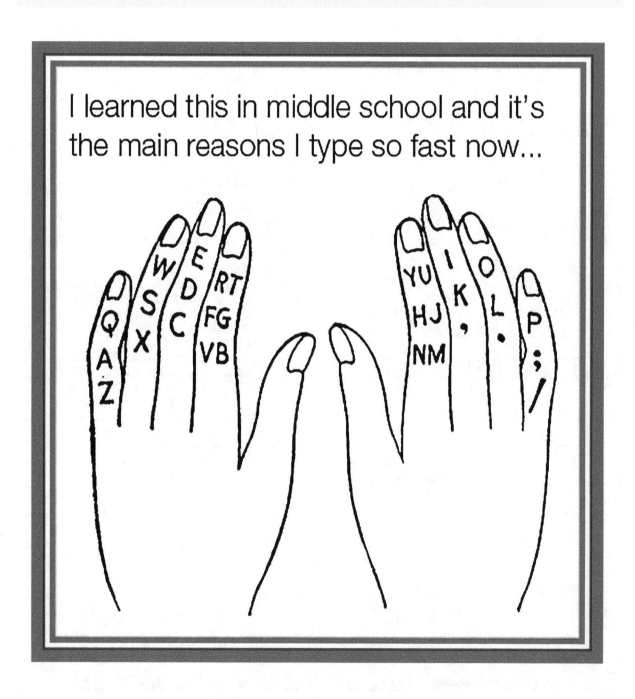

Session 5 Practice Drills To Complete
Typing/Computer Keyboarding Practice Session Diary

Name _____

Lesson #	Completion Date	Start time	Finish time	Typing Lesson Self-Coaching Saying/Quote: What's Yours?
T, S, and L Keys 6				
O, B, and A Keys 7				
V, H, and M Keys 8				
Period and Comma Keys 9				
Beginner Review 2 Self-Check 10				

Session 6

Home Stretch
Website Practice

Did You Know?

Super Typing: If you want to add a bit of entertainment to your typing practice, create your own new long super words to type. Ask friends and family to contribute to your super words list. Then, try to type these super long words. If you type unfamiliar long words like these with speed and accuracy, you most definitely are improving your typing skills.

- **supercalifragilisticexpialidocious** – 34 letters

  a word used when you have nothing to say as in Mary Poppins

- **suparduparextraspectacularbinocularcoloring** – 44 letters

  a word used to describe a fascination with the art of Minnie Evans

Session 6
Good Typing Tip – Speed and Accuracy

What is your desirable speed and accuracy goal at this time? The chart will help you to set a new goal.

Category		Range (WPM)	Mean (WPM)
Kids	Very Slow	<11	-
	Slow	11 – 20	15
	Average	21 – 30	25
	Fast	31 – 40	35
	Very Fast	>40	-
Adults	Very Slow	<26	-
	Slow/Beginner	26 – 35	30
	Intermediate/Average	36 – 45	40
	Fast/Advanced	46 – 65	55
	Very Fast	66 – 80	73
	Insane	>80	-
	Fastest in The World	-	216*
Jobs	Entry Level Clerk/Secretary	35 – 60	-
	Higher/Advanced Level Clerk/Secretary	60 – 80	-
	Data Entry	60 – 80	-
	Dispatch Position/Time Sensitive	80 – 95	-

Session 6 Practice Drills To Complete
Typing/Computer Keyboarding Practice Session Diary

Name _____

Lesson #	Completion Date	Start time	Finish time	Self-Coaching Quote Got a Positive One?
W, X, and : Keys 11				
Q, Y, and P Keys 12				
Z and Enter Keys 13				

Session 7

Wrapping Up
Website Practice

Session 6
Good Typing Tip – Typing Games

Mixing computer typing games into your practice sessions enhances your typing skills development. There are skill building typing games for kids and adults and most of the games are **free**.

The two best things a beginner touch typing gamer can do are to start by mastering the home row keys, first. Next, start with the lower game levels before advancing to the more challenging levels.

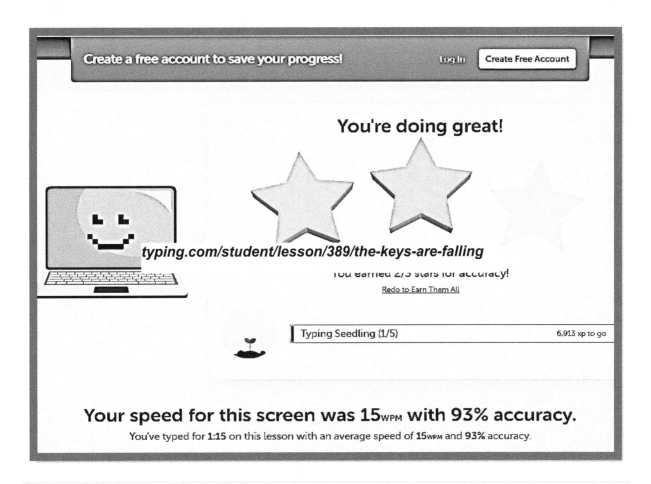

Session 7 Practice Drills To Complete
Typing/Computer Keyboarding Practice Session Diary

Name _____

Lesson #	Completion Date	Start time	Finish time	What emoji or art sticker describes you typing skill development so far?
Beginner Wrap Up Self-Check **14**				
Beginner Assessment **15**				

Session 8

Your
Keyboarding Typing
Certificate

Session 8
Skill Assessment & Your Certificate

- Go to typing.com.
- Select the Typing Speed Test Tab.
- Take at least 2 timed writings.
- **Print a certificate for your best-timed writing**.

Certificate of Accomplishment

This Certification is Hereby Awarded to:

John Q.   Typist

For completion of the official Typing.com timed typing test

1:00 Typing Test

Avg Speed
73 WPM

On the Date of

Avg Accuracy
99%

Verify Save at:
https://www.typing.com/student/verify¥2438244-4349354

Best 3-minute timed writing

Date of Test	Words Per Minute	Errors

Best 5-minute timed writing

Date of Test	Words Per Minute	Errors

Your Typing/Computer Keyboarding Certificate

Print out a hard copy of your certificate. Be sure to save an image of your typing certificate, too.

Place the hard copy of your certificate here.

Session 9

Top 17

Typing Tips & Techniques

Session 9
How to Type Faster and Master the Keyboard

The best 17 tips and techniques to select from that can help enhance your typing skills: Choose 9 that can work for you.

Slow - What really helped me improve my typing speed is slowing down and getting a feel for the keys. First get good at knowing where the keys are then speed up and it will be like riding a bike!

Your Name - My tip to improve your typing speed is to type your name over and over. After that type any word that comes to your mind over and over. If you keep it up you will know a lot of words and suddenly you will find your typing speed shot up.

Music - My tip to improve your typing speed is to just find some music that is fast paced, to your liking, and FUN! After you have found a catchy and fast tune you can start. You'll find your hands vibrating with restlessness. Next thing you know you'll be hitting high speeds and maybe high accuracy with it.

Breathe - My tip is to breathe. If I hold my breath while typing my accuracy decreases, not to mention my WPM. Breathe in and out deeply before beginning the test and be sure to breathe throughout the test. Increasing oxygen to the brain makes the whole body function more accurately...including the fingers!

Pinky Fingers - Everyone says it, but going slow seems to help. I'm working on correcting some bad habits I've developed over 20+ years of typing, and using this site - even for the short time that I have - has been extremely helpful. I'm just going to have to be patient with myself and focus on getting these pinky fingers in the game!

F and J - What helped is I kept on doing the same one until I got the keys down. So, I started on the f and j keys and went forward from there. That is what helped me and I'm only 16 and now I can type at 60 WPM.

15 Minutes - My tip to improve your typing speed is to...practice daily for at least 15 minutes. It has been around 50 days I have started practicing touch typing. It took me at around 15 - 20 days to memorize the keys and then I was able to type without actually looking at the keyboard. My speed was around 5 WPM at that time, and I was constantly practicing daily for about 1 hour, and I gradually increased my typing speed to 9 WPM... 13 WPM... 18 WPM...25 WPM... 31 Wpm. And then actually I started practicing for 15 - 20 minutes daily and today I made it to 32.33 WPM.

It's OK - What really helped me improve my typing speed is... I make sure that I take my time and not to be too hard on myself when I mess up. I learned that self-doubt is your worst enemy and that messing up is okay!

Accuracy First - My tip to improve your typing speed is to concentrate more on accuracy than speed.... It helps much more than increasing your speed.... I've increased my speed by 15 WPM in just 7-10 days in this method.

TV Tray - What really helped me improve my typing speed is typing at a lower table, so that my arms are more level. I put my keyboard on a TV tray whenever possible.

Weakest Key Help - Type out a few paragraphs... note the letters that you are slow writing or often make mistakes with, and DRILL those letters. When speaking of teams, the saying goes ¨We are only as strong as our weakest link¨. Well, I am here to tell you the same concept applies to typing. You are only as fast as your slowest letter.

Common Words - My tip to improve your typing speed is to practice common words. For example, there are many words that have "ing" endings. There are usually common words like and, to, and the. Get into the flow of being able to type common words and endings like these quickly without error.

Mistake Patterns Correction- My tip to improve your typing speed is to... fine the patterns of mistakes that you often make, and improve on those. For me, for whatever reason, it's the word "practice". I always want to make the p, a capital p, even if it's the middle of the sentence. It took a while but the sensation to do so is slowly going away.

Your Activities of Daily Living Fulfillment - My tip to improve your typing speed is to...hey! hi everyone here is the first suggestion I've posted after reading so many! First, I want to say that before I move on which I will, it is important to attend to the details of daily living, fulfilling the roles we've taken on.

Visualize - My tip to improve your typing speed is to...visualize the keyboard in your head to prevent you from looking down at it too often as this slows you down.

Kindergarten - Teach your kids to type at a young age, I learned when I was in kindergarten and they hid the actually placement of the keys so I learned where each letter was by memory.

Touch Type - My tip to improve your typing speed is to learn proper 10-finger touch typing form. The hunt-and-peck method can only go so far, whereas 10 fingers can blaze through text at any speed.

THE AUTHOR

I have taught thousands of people how to type fast and accurate. Karen, who works in a dream career, saw me recently and came over with a big smile to say that the skills and confidence acquired in my digital keyboarding course helps tremendously everyday, especially with her new work from home dream career. Karen tells me that her brilliant son, Carlton, completed my digital keyboarding class, too. Whether you are a student, parent, business owner, developer, Internet user, or absolute beginner, the goal is to have you to complete your own keyboarding activities faster, better, more accurately.

When off work as president of the non-profit--1Byte Computer Literacy, Inc., I periodically publish Bible Friends and Vacation Bible School literature. My favorite hobbie involves serving as a chocolate chip cookie imagineer.

Credits

page 11 pinterest.com

page 12 www.cnet.com

page 15 https://www.elektrenuvsb.lt/

page 16 https://en.wikipedia.org/wiki/Touch_typing

page 22 https://line.17qq.com/articles/odojbdz.html

page 23 pinterest.com

page 25 https://www.teacherspayteachers.com/Product/Keyboarding-Practice-1204159

page 35 https://www.typing-lessons.org/lesson_5.html

page 41 www.speedskin.com

page 47 pinterest.com

page 55 typing.com/student/lesson/389/the-keys-are-falling

page 58 typing.com

pages 60-64 https://www.keyhero.com/wpm-typing-tips/?page=49&lang=0